MY BODY!
What I say GOES!

by **Jayneen Sanders**   illustrated by **Anna Hancock**

A book to empower and teach children about personal body safety, feelings, safe and unsafe touch, private parts, secrets and surprises, consent, and respectful relationships

Note to Caregivers and Educators

In this book children will learn crucial and empowering skills in personal body safety. The book can be read in one sitting but we recommend you return to each page and discuss the concepts with your child after the initial read. Discussion of the various concepts can also occur over a number of sittings. These conversations are ongoing and should happen in general daily interactions with your child. **Please note:** throughout the book we often instruct the child to tell an adult they trust (an adult on their Safety Network) if they feel unsafe. Ensure your child has three to five adults in their life who will listen to and believe them if they come with any concerns. We recommend you have a conversation with your child's chosen, trusted adults so they know how important it is to listen to and believe your child. One trusted adult should not be a family member. There are extensive **Discussion Questions** on pages 38–39 to further draw out the learning.

My Body! What I Say Goes!
Educate2Empower Publishing an imprint of
UpLoad Publishing Pty Ltd
Victoria Australia
www.upload.com.au

First published in 2016

Text copyright © Jayneen Sanders 2016
Illustration copyright © Anna Hancock 2016

Written by Jayneen Sanders
Illustrations by Anna Hancock

Designed by Susannah Low, Butterflyrocket Design

Printed in China through Book Production Solutions

Cataloguing-in-Publication Data
National Library of Australia

Creator: Sanders, Jayneen, author.

Title: My Body! What I Say Goes! : A book to empower and teach children about personal body safety, feelings, safe and unsafe touch, private parts, secrets and surprises, consent, and respectful relationships / by Jayneen Sanders; illustrated by Anna Hancock.

ISBN: 9781925089264 (paperback)

Subjects: Child sexual abuse--Prevention.
Touch.
Personal space.
Individual differences.
Respect for persons.

Other Creators/Contributors: Hancock, Anna, illustrator.

Dewey Number: 362.7672

Disclaimer: The information in this book is advice only written by the author based on her advocacy in this area, and her experience working with children as a classroom teacher and mother. The information is not meant to be a substitute for professional services or advice. For professional help if you are concerned about a child's behavior, go to a health professional and/or contact the key organizations listed at e2epublishing.info/links

Hi! I'm Izzy. In this book you will learn how to keep your body safe, and how to say in a big, strong voice:

This is
MY BODY!
What I say
GOES!

Feelings

Everyone has feelings. You have feelings and I have feelings.

When I'm happy, I have a lovely, warm, fuzzy feeling inside! Sometimes it makes me want to sing. And sometimes it makes me want to dance.

 What do you like to do when you feel happy?

But sometimes I feel sad,
and I want to cry.

You can cry when you are sad.
That's why we have tears.

What makes you feel sad?

This boy is feeling scared.

Why do you think he is feeling scared?

What makes you feel scared?

This girl is feeling angry.

Why do you think she is feeling angry?

What makes you feel angry?

This boy is feeling proud.

Why do you think he is feeling proud?

What makes you feel proud?

261

We all have different kinds of feelings.

Sometimes we feel
HAPPY

...or SAD

...or ANGRY

...or WORRIED

...or SCARED.

It is important to talk about our feelings with adults we trust.

 Who can you talk to about your feelings?

Feeling Safe

At night-time, just before bed, I love to cuddle up on the couch with someone who makes me feel safe and who I trust. We read books and snuggle in close.

I feel safe.

On Saturday mornings, I love to put on my water wings and float in the pool. Dad swims beside me and holds my hand.

I feel safe.

 **When do you feel safe?**

Feeling Unsafe

Sometimes I don't feel safe.

I feel unsafe.

I don't feel safe when Auntie Kate's dog barks at me.

I feel unsafe.

I don't feel safe when Lexi, from next door, pushes me down the slide.

I feel unsafe.

I don't feel safe when one of the older kids at school stands too close to me.

This makes me feel uncomfortable and unsafe.

When I feel unsafe or someone makes me feel uncomfortable,
I know to tell an adult I trust straightaway. If they are too busy or
don't believe me, then I need to tell another trusted adult.

When do you feel unsafe?

Who do you tell?

My Early Warning Signs

When I feel unsafe, my body lets me know. I might have a sick feeling in my tummy or my heart might beat really fast.

♥ BOOM! BOOM! BOOM! ♥

When these things happen to my body,
I call them my Early Warning Signs.

When I feel my Early Warning Signs I know something is not right.
I know I must tell an adult I trust straightaway!

Have you ever felt these Early Warning Signs?
What did you do? Who did you tell?

This boy is feeling unsafe.
There are lots of Early Warning Signs happening to his body.

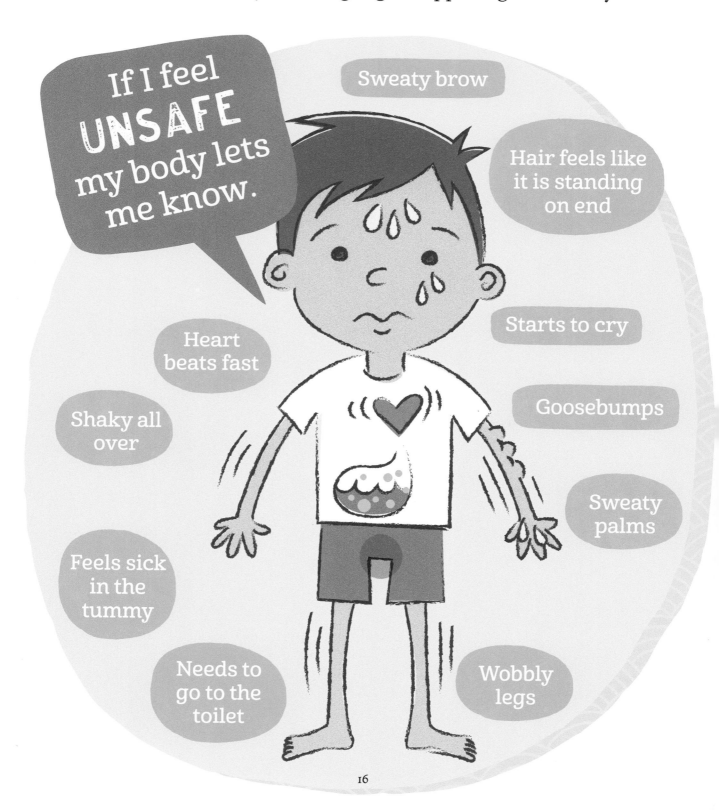

Sometimes you might feel only one or two of your Early Warning Signs and sometimes you might feel all of them.

REMEMBER!
IF YOU FEEL ANY OF YOUR
EARLY WARNING SIGNS,
YOU MUST TELL AN ADULT
YOU TRUST STRAIGHTAWAY!

Can you remember some of
the Early Warning Signs?

My Safety Network

I feel safe! I have a Safety Network.

My Safety Network is made up of five adults who I trust. Anytime I feel unsafe, or I am worried or scared, I can tell one of the adults on my Safety Network. If I can't find that person, I can tell another adult on my Safety Network.

The people on my Safety Network are very important to me, and I am very important to them.

I feel **SAFE!** I have a Safety Network.

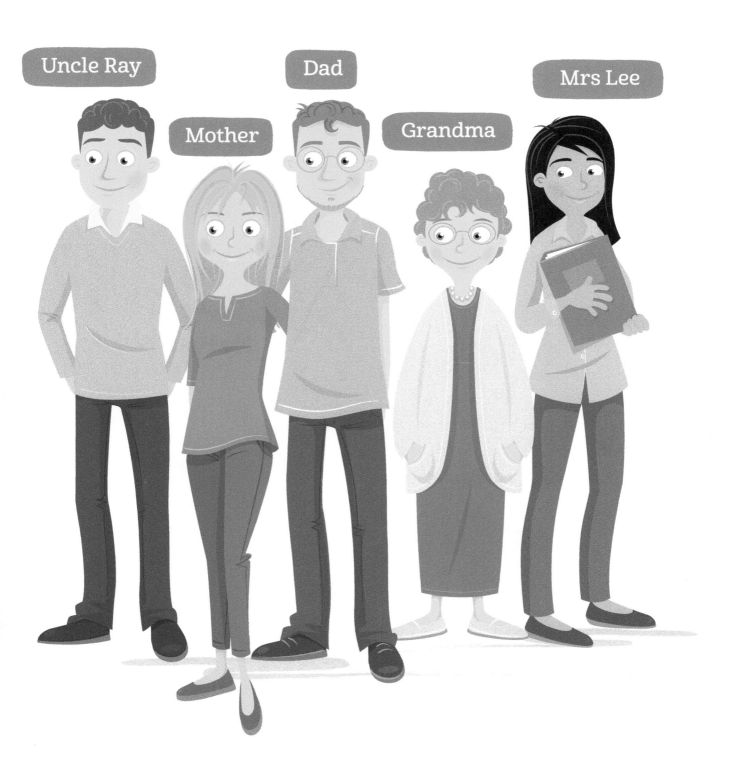

These adults will listen to me when I tell them I feel unsafe
or uncomfortable about something or someone.

Look! I have drawn around my hand. I have written the name of each adult I trust on my Safety Network hand.

Sometimes we don't always have five adults in our lives that we can trust. If you have only three or four people on your Safety Network, that is okay too. One person should not be in your family.

My Safety Network will be different to yours.
You can choose any adults you trust and like.
You can choose an auntie, a teacher,
a grandparent, your mother or father —
anyone who makes you feel safe. It's **your** choice!

Here is my friend Ki's SAFETY NETWORK.

Who will be on your Safety Network?

Private Parts Are Private

We all have bodies. And all our bodies are different.

Some people are tall and some people are short. Some people have blonde hair and some people have black hair.

I have red hair and green eyes.

Ki has brown hair and brown eyes.

We all have private parts. I have private parts and Ki has private parts. My private parts are those parts of my body under my bathing suit or covered by my underwear. Ki's private parts are those parts of his body under his bathing suit or covered by his underwear, too.

Everybody's mouth is a private part. Private means just for you!

People sometimes call our private parts funny names like pee pee or fanny. But we should **always** use the correct names for our private parts.

Boys have a penis, testicles, and a bottom.

Girls have a vulva on the outside and a vagina on the inside. They also have nipples and a bottom. When girls get older the area around their nipples grows into breasts.

These are the **correct** names for our private parts.

No-one should touch your private parts. They belong to **only** you.

When you were a baby, your parents or carer washed and dried your private parts. Now that you are older, you can wash and dry your own private parts because you are the **boss** of your body.

Remember!
It's **your** body! What **you** say goes!

If someone **does** touch your private parts, or asks you to touch their private parts, or shows you pictures of private parts, there are two things you **must** do.

1.

Say in a loud, strong voice with your hand held out, 'Stop! This is **my** body! What I say goes!'

2.

Then go very quickly to a trusted adult on your Safety Network and tell them exactly what happened.

Sometimes if you are sick a doctor might need to check and even touch your private parts. This is only okay if an adult from your Safety Network is with you.

Secrets and Surprises

Surprises are different to secrets. Surprises are things that are happy and fun, and will **always** be told. Secrets can make you feel bad, especially if a person says you must never tell. That's why we don't have secrets in my family. We have happy surprises like not telling Grandpa we are coming to visit, or not telling Uncle Ray about his surprise birthday party.

If someone asks you to keep a secret, tell that person you don't keep secrets. You only keep happy surprises because they will be told.

If someone asks you to keep a secret like touching your private body parts, kissing, or showing you pictures of private parts, you **must** tell an adult on your Safety Network straightaway!

Secrets like those **must** be told! And even if the person tells you not to tell — secrets like those **must** be told!

Body Bubble

We all have an invisible Body Bubble around our body. Invisible means you can't see it ... but it's there!

BODY BUBBLE

Sometimes our **Body Bubble** is called our **BODY BOUNDARY** or **PERSONAL SPACE.**

People should not come inside your Body Bubble if you don't want them too. That's because **your body belongs to you**! If you don't want to kiss or hug someone, you can say politely, 'No, thanks', and then give them a high five or shake their hand instead.

REMEMBER!

It's **your** body! What **you** say goes!

HERE ARE 5 BODY SAFETY RULES TO REMEMBER!

1. MY BODY IS MY BODY

My body is my body and it belongs to me. I can say, 'No!' if I don't want to kiss or hug someone. I can give them a high five or shake their hand.

2. SAFETY NETWORK

I have a Safety Network. These are 3 to 5 adults who I trust. I can tell these people anything and they will believe me. If I feel worried, scared, or uncomfortable, I can tell someone on my Safety Network how I am feeling and why I feel this way.

3. EARLY WARNING SIGNS

If I feel frightened or unsafe, I might feel sick in the tummy or my heart might beat really fast. These feelings are called Early Warning Signs. If I feel this way about anything, I must tell an adult on my Safety Network straightaway.

4. PRIVATE PARTS

I always call my private parts by their correct names. No-one can touch my private parts. No-one can ask me to touch their private parts, and no-one should show me pictures of private parts. If any of these things happen, I must tell a trusted adult on my Safety Network straightaway.

5. NO SECRETS

I don't keep secrets, only happy surprises that will be told. If someone asks me to keep a secret, I tell them I don't keep secrets. If someone asks me to keep a secret that makes me feel unsafe or uncomfortable, I must tell adult on my Safety Network straightaway!

THIS IS MY BODY! WHAT I SAY GOES!

DISCUSSION QUESTIONS
for Parents, Caregivers, and Educators

The following Discussion Questions are intended as a guide, and can be used to initiate an open and empowering dialogue with your child around personal body safety, feelings, safe and unsafe touch, private parts, secrets and surprises, consent, and respectful relationships. The questions are optional and/or can be explored at different readings. I suggest you allow your child time to answer the questions both on the internal pages and in this section, as well, encourage them to ask their own questions around this very important topic. It is equally important that you value their input and listen to their voice. Remain calm and confident discussing this topic with your child as they will take their cues from you. Be prepared to answer any 'challenging' questions from your child. Praise your child's responses and always reassure them of your support. These discussions will help increase your child's skills and knowledge around personal body safety, and will boost their confidence and empowerment.

Pages 4–5
Talk to you child about feeling happy. Ask, 'When do you feel happy? Do you like to dance and sing like Izzy and Super Ted? What do you feel like doing when you are happy?'

Pages 6–9
Discuss other kinds of feelings such as feeling sad, scared, angry, proud, anxious or worried. Ask your child when they feel sad, scared, angry, proud, anxious or worried. For each emotion, ask, 'When you feel xxx, what do you do? Who do you talk to?' Ask, 'Why do you think it is important to talk to someone you trust about how you are feeling?'

Pages 10–11
Ask, 'When do you feel safe? Who makes you feel safe? Why? What kinds of feelings do you have inside when you feel safe?'

Pages 12–13
Ask, 'When do you feel unsafe? Does any person you know make you feel unsafe?' If your child says 'yes', ask them a bit more about that person and why they make your child feel unsafe. Ask, 'What kinds of feelings do you have inside when you feel unsafe? When you feel unsafe, who do you tell? Why do you tell that person?'

Pages 14–15
Ask, 'What is happening in this picture? How do you know Izzy is feeling her Early Warning Signs? Was Izzy right to tell an adult she trusts? How might Izzy feel if she didn't tell anyone?'

Pages 16–17
Discuss the boy on page 16 and talk about his Early Warning Signs. Ask, 'When you feel unsafe, what Early Warning Signs do you get? Sometimes it is okay to feel a little bit scared, like when you go on an exciting ride at a fun park. Have you ever felt a little bit scared in an exciting way? What were you doing? How did your body tell you that you were excited, but a little bit scared? If you feel unsafe in a scared and frightened way, and your Early Warning Signs begin, what should you do straightaway? When have you felt your Early Warning Signs in an unsafe way?'

Pages 18–21
Together with your child, choose three to five adults to be on their Safety Network. Ensure one adult is **not** a family member. Your child will need to feel comfortable with **their** choices. And it is their choice, as 85% of children who reported being sexually abused knew their abuser (*NSW Commission for Children & Young People, 2009*). Your child will also need to feel comfortable that these trusted adults will always believe them if they feel worried or unsafe. Ask your child why the people they have chosen make them feel safe (be mindful of the grooming process; see the book 'Body Safety Education'

for more information on grooming). The adults on your child's Safety Network should be accessible and easy for them to contact when needed. Please check in with each adult before writing their names on your child's safety hand. Make sure they know it is an honor to be chosen, how important they are to your child, and the essential role they play in your child's life. Display your child's safety hand in a prominent place. If you go to *e2epublishing.info* you will find a free safety hand to download, or simply trace around your child's hand. At this point, you could also share a 'safety word'. This is a word your child could say over the phone or anytime to an adult on their Safety Network, and that adult would know your child feels unsafe and the adult needs to act immediately. The word could be anything, e.g. carrots, kangaroo or dinosaur!

Pages 22–25

Discuss the word 'private' as meaning 'just for you'. Talk about private parts as those under a person's bathing suit (or underwear) and name them correctly with your child. **Note:** your child's mouth is also a private part, as are boys' nipples. Explain to your child that even though a boy's nipples are private they are not covered by a bathing suit or underwear. For reasons why we encourage children to learn the correct names for their private parts go to: *e2epublishing.info/blog/2015/10/20/8-reasons-not-to-call-your-childs-genitals-these-pet-names* At this time, you may also like to introduce the word 'public'. Talk about our 'public' body parts as those that we all see such as our ears, nose, and arms (but not the mouth). You could also relate 'private' and 'public' to places such as a toilet being a private place and a kitchen being a public place. Reassure your child that it is okay for them to touch their own private parts (as it can feel good) but only in a private place such as their own bedroom. If you wish to show your child appropriate drawings of private parts to discuss the difference between boys and girls anatomically, you can download free age-appropriate line drawings of children's private parts at *e2epublishing. info* under Parents.

Pages 26–27

Discuss that babies and toddlers need their private parts washed by their carers but once a child is older they can do this by themselves. Point out that your child's own trusted carer/s can dry their body but only if they feel comfortable with this.

Pages 28–29

Ask, 'What must you do if you are touched on your private parts?' Have your child rehearse exactly what they need to do, as on page 28. **Note:** sometimes a child may not feel confident or may be too young to say, 'No' as the perpetrator is someone they know well. Ensure they understand that if they don't feel confident to say 'No' they should go straight to point 2 and tell someone on their Safety Network straightaway. Talk about how sometimes a doctor may need to touch their private parts if they are sick, but only if an adult from their Safety Network is present. Discuss other situations such as a person asking your child to touch their private parts or look at images of private parts. Ask, 'What must you do if this happens?'

Pages 30–33

Ask, 'What do you think is the difference between a surprise and a secret? What should you do if someone asks you to kept a secret? Has anyone asked you to keep a secret that made you feel bad or uncomfortable? Has anyone asked you to keep a secret that made you experience your Early Warning Signs? What did you do?' Look at the picture on page 33. Ask, 'What do you think the older boy is doing? Is the younger boy right to run away? How do you think the younger boy is feeling? Where do you think he is going?'

Pages 34–37

Ask, 'Do you always have to kiss or hug another person if you don't want to? Just because an adult asks you for a kiss or a hug, does that mean you have to kiss or hug them? What could you do instead?' For an excellent children's book on this topic read, 'No Means No!' available at e2epublishing.info Discuss how it is best to ask a person's permission if we wish to hug or kiss them, and even though parts of our bodies are 'public', it does not mean people can come inside our Body Bubble without our consent. Point out that a dentist or doctor needs to ask permission if they wish to look inside a person's mouth. Lastly, encourage your child to stand firm; legs slightly apart (like a proud pirate or superhero) and say in a strong voice, 'This is MY body! What I say goes!'

BOOKS BY THE SAME AUTHOR

Some Secrets Should Never Be Kept

'Some Secrets Should Never Be Kept' is an award-winning and beautifully illustrated children's book that sensitively broaches the subject of inappropriate touch. This book was written as a tool to help parents, caregivers, and teachers broach the subject with children in an age-appropriate and non-threatening way. Suitable for children 3 to 11 years.

No Means No!

'No Means No!' is a children's picture book about an empowered little girl who has a very strong and clear voice in all issues, especially those relating to her body. This book teaches children about personal boundaries, respect, and consent; empowering kids by respecting their choices and their right to say, 'No!' Suitable for children 2 to 9 years.

No Difference Between Us

A book to empower children and teach them from the earliest of years about gender equality, respectful relationships, feelings, choice, self-esteem, empathy, tolerance, and acceptance. Suitable for children 2 to 9 years.

Pearl Fairweather, Pirate Captain

Captain Pearl Fairweather is a brave, fair, and strong pirate captain. She and her diverse crew of twenty-four women sail the seven seas on the good ship, *Harmony*. All is well, until the day Captain Sandy McCross sails into their lives and demands to take over Pearl's ship! This beautifully illustrated children's book sets out to empower young girls to be strong, assertive, self-confident, and self-reliant, and for boys to respect that empowerment, and to embrace and value it. Suitable for children 5 to 12 years.

Body Safety Education
A parents' guide to protecting kids from sexual abuse

This essential and easy-to-read guide contains simple, practical, and age-appropriate ideas on how parents, carers and educators can protect children from sexual abuse — ensuring they grow up as assertive and confident teenagers and adults.

CPSIA information can be obtained
at www.ICGtesting.com
Printed in the USA
BVHW020538270621
610343BV00005B/24

9 781925 089264